HELP FOR YOUR DARKEST TIME

HELP FOR YOUR DARKEST TIME

JONATHAN SHUTTLESWORTH

Released June 2024
eBook ISBN: 978-1-64457-300-6
Paperback ISBN: 978-1-64457-301-3

Rise UP Publications
644 Shrewsbury Commons Ave, Ste 249
Shrewsbury PA 17361
United States of America
www.riseUPpublications.com
Phone: 866-846-5123

CONTENTS

There is a way out of every problem.

— JONATHAN SHUTTLESWORTH

.

INTRODUCTION

I pray this will be a blessing and a tool of deliverance for every man and woman going through the hardest time they've ever had and who doesn't know what to do, doesn't see a way out, and is discouraged by the Enemy. I pray the Lord will use what I've written to restore their hope and empower them with faith to come out of the pit they're in right now and get through the darkest time of their life.

What do you do when you're going through the darkest time of your life?

I'd been preaching in Barbados with my cousin Teddy. He had preached the night before and went through the seven names of God—Jehovah-Jireh, Jehovah Rapha, and down the line—and taught on each briefly. Then he told everyone, "Whatever you need God to be for you right now, begin to call on that name and worship Him." So, the whole crowd did.

The next night was the last night. When a meeting ends, people often ask if they can take pictures or have their Bibles signed. A lady came to me and said, "The meetings have been such a blessing to me."

I asked, "How so?"

She responded, "I had no food in my refrigerator, and we're four months behind on our rent." It was just her and her daughter. She continued, "When Ted taught on the names of God and said, 'Call on what you need God to be for you,' I began to call on Him as Jehovah-Jireh and worship Him as Jehovah-Jireh and that He would meet all our needs. The next morning, the landlord came to evict us." She went on, "Me and my daughter, we had no place to go. But when he came to evict us, the expression on his face changed, and he gave us money."

She was four months behind in rent, and not only did he give them money, but the landlord came back an hour later with six bags of groceries. She said, "My daughter and I just began to cry." I'll never forget when she said to her daughter, "See, honey, what the preacher said is true. God took care of us. Mommy didn't have to defile her body to get rent money or to get food for us." She said joyfully, "I've been thanking God all day."

If you're a minister, always remember there are struggling people in your church. If you do, you'll never preach boring sermons. Your heart of compassion will be evident when you understand that some people are going through very dark times; maybe they're months behind on rent, have no food, or have experienced a profound loss or disappointment. Teddy and I weren't preaching in central Africa, we were right in the Caribbean—not in a third-world nation. To a greater or lesser degree, there are people like this in every meeting you have as a minister. After hearing that lady's testimony, it was all I could do to hold back my tears. I renewed my commitment to make sure my ministry is geared toward people going through terrible things. When you walk in victory as a minister like I do, you must remember this reality—it's challenging to do.

When I share the testimony of our ministry receiving $1.1 million, it never gets anywhere near the response as when I tell about a time my grandparents ran out of food and God answered my grandma's prayer by sending 21 chickens marching down the hill to lay eggs every morning. Do you know why? Most people aren't entrepreneurs. Most people aren't believing for million-dollar things. Most people live hand to mouth, believing in God for their next meal. The Bible is for everybody, but most people are not believing for God to expand their business or to buy a second home.

People are mostly just trying to get through life. There are many people—more than I think the average minister realizes—who are going through extremely dark and difficult times. Maybe as you read this book, you're facing a situation for which there's no easy answer: your husband is abusive, you have a child who's on heroin—those kinds of things. You don't need somebody giving you a glib, Christian cliché. "Hang in there, everything happens for a reason. I'll be praying for you." That's not going to get the job done.

I'm writing this book because I want to provide something substantial to hurting people who need to know what to do.

I'm sure many people reading this have gone through much worse things than I have, but I want to share two very dark times in my life. One helped me relate to people who are sick. Before this experience, if somebody had stage four cancer and was bedridden—yellow eyes and 80 pounds—I used to tell their family, "Bring them into my meetings so they can hear the Word." But after I went through what I did, I realized that it doesn't really work when you're at death's door.

In 2014, I joined the Redeemed Christian Church of God on their 100-day fast. It was a 100-day fast, from 6:00 AM to 6:00 PM. However, if you completed 30 straight days of fasting without breaking, it counted as the whole 100 days. Since I usually did 21 days without breaking anyway, I decided to do 30 days, as did my pastor, and it was fine. It was one of the easiest, best fasts I've ever been on. When I broke my fast, I broke it properly. I broke it with a small portion of rice and some seafood. I didn't eat much, probably a fifth of a normal portion. I took the leftovers to my hotel room and put them in the refrigerator.

Later, I preached, and when I returned to my hotel, I ate the leftovers. When I took the first bite, it didn't taste right. I had just brushed my teeth, so I thought maybe it was the toothpaste or something. I took maybe four or five more bites, then I gave up on it; something didn't taste right.

Those five bites gave me the worst case of food poisoning I've ever had. Usually, you can just fight through food poisoning. The problem was that I had not eaten in 30 days, other than having that small meal. Now I couldn't keep anything down—not even water. Everything I put in my mouth, I immediately vomited. This lasted for several days. I was already weak from the fast, and for another seven days, I couldn't even hold water. I'm not overstating it. I recognize now that this was an attack from the Devil because, in that moment, I felt like ol' Jon was going home to be with the Lord.

I didn't go to the hospital because I'd already made up my mind that I would never go to one. When I got back to Pittsburgh, I shut the door and went to sleep. I stayed in bed for five or six straight days. I was getting worse every day. This is why I now understand people who are at death's door, because I know a bit of how it feels. You don't feel like doing anything. You're not interested in anything. You have no life. I didn't feel well enough to pray. I didn't feel able to resist. I wasn't worried. I was just dead-like. Now I understand when I meet people who need prayer and they're unresponsive, they can't sit and listen for an hour in a meeting. They don't even have the energy to pay attention. It's as if nothing matters. I understand these things now.

The way the Lord brought me out of my situation is pretty interesting, and it gave me a newfound love for God and how good He is in a time of weakness. When I was lying there at death's door, my mother called me one morning from her home in Maine and asked, "Jonathan, are you okay?"

In a weakened voice, I answered, "I'm fine," because I will never say otherwise.

She said, "Well, all I'm going to tell you is the Lord woke me out of a dead sleep last night, and I felt the most urgent need to pray for you that I've ever felt. I prayed all through the night and this morning"—it was getting close to noontime. She continued, "I felt like you were at the point of death, and I wanted to call you."

I responded, "Well, thank you for praying for me."

My father, who was in Toronto at the time, called me right after my mother hung up. He didn't know anything about what she had said; they hadn't spoken.

My dad told me, "I felt to pray for you last night, and I've been praying for you all day." Since he brought it up, I told him what happened, and he prayed with me over the phone.

That was when I began to mend. I'm thankful that God mobilized people to help me and care for me when I was too weak to pray. In about 24 hours, I came out of it. But I now understand what it's like to knock on death's door. When your mind is shut down, you don't have the energy to think or engage in anything. You don't care about your own life when you're at that point—you resign to death. I got a taste of that and gained greater compassion for people in similar situations.

The second darkest time of my life happened after I had preached about five times in 36 hours, twice in Allentown, Pennsylvania, and three services in Harrisburg, Pennsylvania. My wife was nauseated and didn't seem herself that afternoon. She had been on the road with me the entire week, so I told her to stay at the hotel and rest. It wasn't a big deal for her to miss the Sunday night service. We were in services all week, twice a day. I wanted her to rest until she felt better. I left her in our hotel room with Camila, our daughter, and I went to preach that night's service, and we had a great service.

Camila was playing when I returned to our hotel room, but Adalis was in the bathroom. I called to her but got no response. I thought she couldn't hear me because the fan was on. After a while, I opened the door and found Adalis slumped over the toilet with her head resting on the toilet paper roll. She was unconscious, her lips white, and the toilet was full of blood. Later, the doctors told us she had hemorrhaged and lost about 37% of her blood. She was almost dead. I pulled her off the toilet and slapped her face to wake her up. I laid her on the bed, laid on top of her, and commanded life to come back into her body. It was a horrid thing to experience. While I was doing that, Camila, who was only about two years old at the time, was playing and watching cartoons in the background.

As I laid Adalis down, I didn't know what happened to her or how much blood she had lost. I only knew the toilet was full of blood. As I prayed for her, she drifted in and out of consciousness. I prayed throughout the night. I was exhausted. After preaching five times in the last 36 hours, I didn't have any energy left. I think that's why I was able to remain calm, because I didn't have enough energy to panic.

I made up my mind to preach the 8:00 AM service the next morning. Some people may think it was cruel, but I asked myself, 'What would the Devil want me to do in this situation?' I concluded he'd want me to lay by my wife and cry and hold her hand. I had already prayed the best I knew how. I told the Lord, "At eight years old, before I ever married this woman, I made a commitment to You to preach. I can't heal my wife, so I'm going to do what you called me to do and trust you to take care of my wife."

I felt the Lord give me an idea. I called a lady named Astrid Soni from the Democratic Republic of the Congo. She was in asylum in the United States. She's a powerful woman of God. I called her, and she came and prayed for Adalis. I told her what had happened. She stayed by her bed, prayed for her in tongues, and made her kale soup to help increase her iron levels. I left and preached that morning on joy and healing. I preached on everything I knew the Devil wouldn't want me to preach.

Adalis didn't come out of that in a day or even three days. She remained anemic and weak for about eight months. It took about 13 months until she was back to herself.

I'm not claiming what I experienced was the worst thing anybody's ever gone through. Dr. Rodney Howard-Browne had to bury his daughter after she died on Christmas day. For many years, his daughter was in and out of intensive care, getting lung treatments, and he had to tear himself away from the intensive care unit to preach to people—that's totally amazing. I'm writing this book for people going through something like that, where there's no easy answer.

My ministry is increasing at such a rapid pace because I always search for logical answers to problems that arise. Most problems have a quick remedy, but what about somebody going through something without a logical, quick, or easy answer? What do you do when you're going through the darkest time of your life?

I want to give you six things that are not Christian clichés or glib statements, but six things to keep in your spirit, and a few things you can do to help you through the darkest times of your life and come out on top. Both situations I mentioned are over—we're not dealing with them anymore. You can go through the valley of the shadow of death and come out on the other side. I want you to know that whatever you're going through is not final.

Dr. Rodney's daughter is in Heaven. He's not strung out on medication, and his wife isn't loaded up with antidepressants. Today, they're doing more than ever in the ministry to stick it to the Devil. You can see what God's done with Adalis, and you can see what God's done through me. I not only want to relate to you, but I also want to be an example to you. Whatever you're going through, the story is not over.

> **Whatever you're going through, the story is not over.**

When people read the book of Job, they often wallow in the part where he's going through his problems, but his problem lasted 18 months out of a long life. When he came through the other side, the Lord restored double for all the enemy had stolen. Job lived another 70 years afterward and had twice as much as the enemy stole.

Remember, there's a way out of every problem. You will come through this. I want God to use this book to bring you out of it in Jesus' name.

CHAPTER ONE

UNDERSTAND THAT GOD IS GOOD

Every good gift and every perfect gift is from
above, and comes down from the Father of
lights, with whom there is no variation or
shadow of turning.

— JAMES 1:17 (NKJV)

God is not the author of your problem. Thinking
that God is the creator of your problem is what
screwed Job up, but it wasn't really his fault because he
didn't have a Bible. Job thought God was attacking
him. He didn't realize it was the Devil who attacked his
life. He said, *"The Lord has given, and the Lord has taken
away,"* (Job 1:21) without realizing the Lord hadn't
taken anything away from him.

The way out of your problem is by the hand of God. God supernaturally touched my wife. God supernaturally touched my body and mobilized my parents to pray for me when I was too weak to pray. When you're going through the hardest time of your life, only the hand of God will bring you out. One of the things the Devil wants to do is get you to blame God, to be angry at God, or see God as having allowed the thing or brought it into your life. If Satan can turn you against God, then he has successfully turned you against any hope you have of getting out of your problem. Your problem doesn't come from God.

> The thief does not come except to steal, and to
> kill, and to destroy. I have come that they
> may have life, and that they may have it more
> abundantly.

— JOHN 10:10 (NKJV)

The Lord is good, and His mercy endures forever. Either indirectly or directly, the problems you have come from the Devil. Don't ever get confused and think God sends problems your way. That's why I attack any minister or ministry that says things like, "Well, sometimes God gives us the good times, but He also gives us the bad times." No, it's not God. It wasn't God who gave me food poisoning. That was an attack from the Enemy in an attempt to take me out. It wasn't

God who caused my wife to hemorrhage and miscarry our child; it was the Devil.

You must view the Devil as the author of your problems and recognize it's God who holds the supernatural power to deliver you from them. That's how Job gained restoration. He knew God's hand was his way out. It was his wife who said, *"Are you going to remain faithful after all this? Curse God and die!"* To which Job replied, *"you talk like a foolish woman. Though He slay me, yet will I trust Him?"* (Job 2:9-10). That's the point you must get to: "God, I'm yours forever. I will never back out of the covenant I have with you. I love you. I belong to you."

That's why I preached three times when my wife was lying on what could have been her deathbed. I'm never going to back out of my covenant with God. When you stay close to God during the darkest times of your life, you'll discover God will never back out on His covenant with you.

> The Lord will stay with you as long as you stay with him! Whenever you seek him, you will find him. But if you abandon him, he will abandon you.
>
> — 2 CHRONICLES 15:2

Ultimately, the Devil does these things to push you away from God. Sometimes, when a pastor dies or backslides, the wife stops going to church because she's mad at God. That anger is the Devil continuing his attack in an attempt to destroy an entire family. He's not content to kill, he keeps working to get the wife to go to Hell. Then eventually, the children will go to Hell. Instead of people drawing closer to God in times of trouble, they pull away from God, causing their own destruction.

The way to stop the darkest hour of your life is to draw near to God, for He will lift you up in the time of trouble. *"God is our refuge and strength, a very present help in trouble"* (Psalms 46:1). God is good. God is not the author of your trouble. I feel the anointing on this for people reading right now. Maybe you're struggling with a lousy marriage or children who have abandoned the morals and values you raised them to have. Don't allow these things to push you away from God and toward alcohol, marijuana, or prescription pills; it's time to press into God. The Bible says that when David was hunted by King Saul, he went and found the prophet Samuel and took refuge in the prophet's house (1 Samuel 19:18). David found the anointing in his time of trouble. When Saul sent more people to kill him, the power of God hit them and knocked them on their backs—they couldn't get near him.

God is not the author of the problem—He is your way out of the problem.

My friend, whatever hard thing you're going through, it's not time to pull away from God. It's time to draw near to God more than you ever have. That's your way out. You'll never get away from God. It's time to throw yourself on the mercy of God, and God will help you in your time of trouble. *"The name of the Lord is a strong tower; the righteous run to it and are safe"* (Proverbs 18:10). Remember, God is good. Run to Him.

CHAPTER TWO

DON'T BEAT YOURSELF UP

W hen people attempt to find a reason for why things are going wrong, it solidifies the problem. If you can identify a practical reason for your problem, you should. But when I was ill from food poisoning, that wasn't the time for me to wonder what I did wrong. Instead, I asked the Lord for mercy.

When I pray with people who are going through a hard time, I've noticed a common thread that keeps them stuck in their problems for a long time: they continually beat themselves up. They'll say, "I could've done more. I didn't do this, or I should have done that. What am I doing wrong? Do I not have enough faith? Is my confession wrong?" Look, if it is on you, then ask the Lord to forgive you. But you're not going through a difficult time because you're a bad person. You're going through what you're going through because the Bible says, *"The earth lieth in wickedness"* (1 John 5:19). There's a real devil who *"walks about like a roaring lion, seeking whom he may devour"* (1Peter 5:8).

The Enemy came after me and he came after my wife. It wasn't our fault. We didn't bring it upon ourselves. There are steps we can take to secure our shield of faith to ensure it never happens again, but when you're in the midst of a challenge, it's not the time to identify how it happened. It's the time to thank God for His goodness and throw yourself on His mercy. Ask Him for help, and if need be, forgiveness.

Don't beat yourself up.

If your 14-year-old is on heroin, your 17-year-old does meth, and your 19-year-old went to university and totally backslid, it's not the time to analyze the last 18 years. Don't waste time thinking about what a horrible mother or father you are or what you could have done better. It's time to throw yourself on the mercy of God and say, "Father, I'm sure I could have been a better dad. I'm sure I could have been a better mother, but I need your help right now. I don't want my child to go to Hell. Bring them out of this."

The Enemy wants you to blame yourself and get a two-for-one deal. He wants your kid to be on heroin, and for you to be on antidepressants with dark mascara under your eyes, looking like you're going through the throes of death. He wants you sitting alone in a room all day, beating yourself up about what you could've done better. When you're going through the valley of the shadow of death, that's not the time to ask what you could have done better in 1992. Instead, it's the time to say, "Yes, I'm sure I wasn't perfect, but God, I need your help right now." This keeps it from being a decades-long ordeal and makes it something you can get past more immediately.

In the book of Job, the Devil didn't just attack Job's life. He also sent Job's "friends" to accuse him and make him aware of what he might have done to deserve the attack. Christians can be the worst friends. For every preacher who dies, ten other faith preachers come up with reasons why the guy died—people are great at finding reasons after the fact.

When people come to me at the altar and say, "I have this that's going wrong. Why do you think it's going wrong? Do you think it's because of this?" I simply reply, "Who cares? Let's pray and take care of it."

The Bible tells us the Word will teach us, point out what's wrong, and correct us. So, whatever you've done wrong, God will point it out to you as you stay in the Word. God will not allow you, as His child, to keep going down the wrong road. If you stay in the Word, it won't happen again. But when you're going through the valley of the shadow of death, it's not the time to question yourself and beat yourself up. Just attack the problem and say, "Problem, however you came, you can go back to Hell, in Jesus' name."

God is not creating problems to teach you a lesson. Do you think the Lord caused your daughter to become addicted to heroin so that you can realize what a lousy mother you are? No. The Devil is the accuser of the brethren (Revelation 12:10). God is not using the tragedy you're going through right now to point out the flaws in your life. That's what the Devil wants you to think. The Devil uses it like that, but God is a good God, and God is not the author of the problem. So don't beat yourself up, even if it was your fault.

> **Even if something is your fault, God can make up for your error if you allow Him.**

You could be a 43-year-old woman who was saved last year, with a daughter in her twenties who's having all kinds of problems. You didn't raise her in church, but that's where the mercy of God comes in. This is when you say, "Father, I didn't know you when I was a young mother or father, but I know you now. I ask you now to make up for my failures and restore my family to me. Just like Paul told the jailer that his house will be saved, bring salvation to my household to make up for the lost years."

God can make up for your errors. My father-in-law is an excellent example of this. He didn't serve the Lord for much of his life, but when my mother-in-law was pregnant with twins, he prayed, "Father, make up for all the wasted years I had by using these two girls in the ministry." Fast-forward to today: one girl is my wife, Adalis, and the other is Magalis, who runs our entire ministry.

CHAPTER THREE

YOUR LIFE HAS TREMENDOUS VALUE

> For we are God's masterpiece. He has created us
> anew in Christ Jesus, so we can do the good
> things he planned for us long ago.
>
> — EPHESIANS 2:10

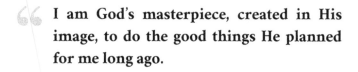

**I am God's masterpiece, created in His
image, to do the good things He planned
for me long ago.**

I can't stand to hear preachers say, "We're nothing; God is everything." That's not true. You're created in the image of God. You matter. You're God's masterpiece. You've been placed on Earth by God as a solution to the problems the Enemy is plaguing mankind with.

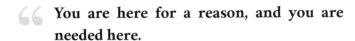 **You are here for a reason, and you are needed here.**

When I had food poisoning, I learned what it's like to think, 'I've had a good run, I'm tired, I'm worn out, I might as well go to Heaven now.' Elijah, one of the mightiest prophets to ever live, felt the same way. He sat under a tree and said, "God, take me to Heaven. I'm no better than anybody else." You must come against this thinking and realize you have exceptional value.

> He sat down under a solitary broom tree and prayed that he might die. "I have had enough, Lord," he said. "Take my life, for I am no better than my ancestors who have already died."
>
> — 1 KINGS 19:4

God placed you on this earth for a good reason. As the Holy Ghost anoints you, you bring something unique into this earth—something only you can bring. The more clearly you understand your value, the better soul-winner you will be. You're not just bringing someone to the Lord so they can go to Heaven instead of Hell. When they get saved, grounded, and rooted in the things of God, they'll also become a powerful force in the Kingdom of God. When you understand your value, you realize the Kingdom of God will lack something without your life. People have value. Every soul you win is like a fish you catch with a gold coin in its mouth. They will add something to the Kingdom of God. God has placed something unique within you. As you connect with the anointing, you will make an impact on the earth.

Don't ever let the Devil make you think your life is inconsequential, that you've had your day, or that no one cares about you. Don't allow the Devil to cause you to question when your children last called, or the last time somebody came to visit you—none of it matters.

You're created in the image of God. I'm telling you—as someone who matters—that you matter. The world will be worse off without you and better with you in it. This revelation will restore the fight in you. Don't be done. You have all of eternity to be in Heaven, so don't take your life. Come against any thought of suicide. You matter. You have an impact to make on people. Don't give the Devil the satisfaction of seeing you check out early. Fight for your life. You have all of eternity to be in Heaven; you have a short time to be here on Earth, and the Kingdom of God needs you here.

CHAPTER FOUR

SURROUND YOURSELF WITH THE WORD OF GOD

W hen you're weak and fighting for your life, you're in no position to look up podcasts or sermons. That's why we made the Revival Today app, providing 24/7 access to the preaching of the Word of God. *"The Word of God is living and active, sharper than any two-edged sword,"* and it carries quickening power. (Hebrews 4:12). The Bible says in Romans chapter four, that Abraham believed the Word of God and his body grew strong and became empowered by faith.

> The Spirit of God, who raised Jesus from the dead, lives in you. And just as God raised Christ Jesus from the dead, he will give life to your mortal bodies by this same Spirit living within you.
>
> — ROMANS 8:11

If you listen to anointed preaching, like one of my sermons, or somebody else who carries anointing for preaching—even when your body is too tired to care—it will quicken your spirit. The Bible says it will quicken your mortal body. The Word of God carries healing virtue in it. If you're going through something right now, or if the Enemy attacks in the future and you don't know what to do, turn on our app. It's not going to feed your depression. It's not going to give you a soundtrack to listen to as you go down to the grave. You will hear anointed preaching that fires up your spirit and lifts you out of your situation.

> **Listening to anointed preaching brings strength to your body.**

Don't allow the atmosphere around you to become depressing. Don't allow yourself to sulk with your blinds drawn, lights turned low, sad music playing, and Lifetime Movie Network on in the background—even though you feel like it. You can tell an attack is demonic when such things become attractive.

Isn't it interesting how when you're going through an attack, your flesh craves listening to some kind of depressing, sad music? You actually don't want to listen to preaching, especially somebody like me. Isn't it interesting how people only want to listen to a preacher like me when things are going well? The

Devil doesn't want you listening to somebody like me when you're under attack—you need to do the opposite of what he wants. Put on what you don't feel like listening to. Don't put on things that feed your depression and sadness. Listen to somebody who will stir your spirit and quicken your body by the power of God.

Surround yourself with the Word of God.

CHAPTER FIVE

YOU NEED TO BE AROUND CONQUERORS

You don't need to listen to people who are going through the same thing as you. When facing a situation in life, it's your flesh that desires to seek out others who share your experience. Two people in a pit can't help each other out of the pit. But someone who's climbed out of the pit can reach down and pull the other one up. You need to seek out people who have not only faced the challenge you have but who have faced it and conquered it.

If you have a child on drugs, don't find other parents with children on drugs and talk about how hard it is to go through that ordeal. People facing similar problems are ill-equipped to help you. They can't lift you up, and you can't lift them up. Find somebody who had a child on drugs and, by the power of God, saw them delivered. Listen to what they did and allow their testimony to inspire you.

> **Find people who have conquered situations like your own and allow their testimony to inspire you to come out of your own situation.**

Don't join yourself with fellow oppressed people. Solidarity in suffering may provide some comfort, but it does little to solve the problem. Find people who are more than conquerors and victors, and let their testimonies and stories inspire you to come out of whatever you are going through.

CHAPTER SIX

GOD HAS PROMISED ALL THINGS WILL WORK TOGETHER FOR GOOD...

And we know that God causes everything to
work together for the good of those who
love God and are called according to his
purpose for them.

— ROMANS 8:28

"All things will work together for the good of
those who love God and are called according
to His purpose." *All* things. God said that, and *"God is
not a man that He should lie"* (Numbers 23:19). If God
said it, He'll perform it. This doesn't mean God sent the
bad things. It means God causes the attack sent by the
Devil to be turned around and used for your good. God
did the same for Joseph. Everything went against
Joseph, and God worked it all out so that Joseph ended
up way better off than before the attack came.

I prophesy, in the name of Jesus, that as you are reading this and as you open your heart to the Spirit of God, God will supernaturally reverse what you're going through right now and make the Devil pay you back double for everything he took. As He did for Job—who was under a worse covenant—He'll do better for you under a new and better covenant, built on better promises. All things work together for good.

I prophesy that everyone reading this, whatever you're going through, God will see to it that at the end of the story, you're twice as better off as before it started. You don't have to know how it will happen; you just have to believe God will do it. For all the sorrows and tears the Enemy brought into your life, God will do something where your mouth will be filled with laughter and your tongue with singing. If you lose sight of this and lose your hope, you're a dead man. You're a dead woman. You must keep yourself in check, like Job amid his problem, *"I know my Redeemer lives."* You need to say, "God, I don't know how, but I believe you're going to work this out where I come up higher and better than before this attack came."

I want to share the outcomes of those two stories I opened with in the introduction to illustrate how God worked things together for good and turned them around to make my circumstances better than before the attacks. The first one was when I had food poisoning. After my parents prayed for me, I got out of bed and went to vomit even though I had nothing left to vomit. I kneeled down, grabbed both sides of the toilet, and heaved. After the third heave, my back cracked.

Those who've known me for a while know I used to be nearly crippled. People would wait for me with a wheelchair when I was getting off airplanes, despite not having ever requested a wheelchair. You know you're crippled when people send wheelchairs for you without bothering to ask if you need one.

> **He will use the problems for your good if you allow Him.**

When I puked that third time, my back popped, and it felt good. Before that moment, I had ripped all the towel racks off the walls of any bathroom Adalis and I had ever had, using them to pull myself up. I couldn't get up from a kneeling position without using my arms—I had no strength in my legs or back. But when my back popped, I felt strength come to my legs. I stood up without using my hands, which I had never done before. I walked out, and it was one of the funniest scenes. The Lord will fill your mouth with laughter, and He'll often find an amusing way to do it.

I had been in such pain that the only way I could sleep was to knock myself out with NyQuil, but then I would vomit it up. So, I had blue NyQuil drool from my face to my underwear. Adalis came into the room because she heard me laughing. There I was, sickly and bone-thin at 140 pounds, laughing, with blue drool snaking down to my underwear. Adalis probably thought I was going home to be with the Lord, losing my mind. She asked me what I was laughing about. I told her, "The Devil tried to kill me, but instead, I got a free chiropractic adjustment, and my back is better." Then she started laughing, half at what I said and half at how ridiculous I looked. The problems cleared up. Not only did God heal me of the food poisoning I was attacked with, but He also healed my back—that's double for the attack.

I'm telling you, if you are going through the hardest time of your life, God is not only going to bring you out of the attack, He's going to give you a blessing for your trouble. The thief must refund double for everything he stole (Exodus 22:7).

Remember, God doesn't send the bad. God takes what the Enemy meant for bad and turns it for good. After Adalis had a miscarriage and hemorrhage, she didn't just recover. While Adalis was facing her problem, she began listening to Kenneth Copeland, Andrew Wommack, and Bishop Oyedepo, for at least three hours each day. Well, do you know what happened? Her intake of the Word strengthened her enough to propel her out of her situation and become healthier than she'd ever been. But it also put an overflow of the

Word in her that continues to bubble out of her to this day.

I remember riding in the car with her as she was talking. She'd been talking for about 30 minutes when I realized it felt exactly like riding with my father or with Teddy or with Dr. Rodney—it was a preacher talking. That's when I told her I was going to have her speak at our next meeting. I knew she was ready. Her video devotionals (vidotionals) came after that. The vidotionals have been seen across the continent of Africa and on national television in the United States. Our ministry's women's conference—and much more—was birthed out of the vidotionals. Now she preaches at her own meetings. What the Devil hit my wife with drove her to God and to His Word. Not only did God bring her out, but she came out as a superwoman. She's 10 times the woman she was before the attack.

I prophesy to all men and women who are reading this right now, not only will you come out of the attack you're under, but you'll also come out 10 times the man or woman you are right now, in Jesus' name.

Pray this prayer out loud: Father, in the name of Jesus, I pray that you would bring me out of my current situation right now. I curse every invisible force that's working to steal, kill, and destroy my life. Let today mark the end of all my struggles. Pick me up out of the pit and set my feet on the rock to stand, in Jesus' name. I thank you and give you praise. I thank you that you are true to your Word, and not only will you deliver me from my problem, but you'll cause the Devil to pay double for what he stole from me. In the mighty name of Jesus, Amen.

Now, lift at least one hand, and out of your own mouth, begin to thank God right now. Although He is with you through the valley of the shadow of death, He's not there to camp with you. He's walking you through and out of that place, in Jesus' name. This is not a year for you to struggle and be under attack, this is a year for you to prosper and increase. Any hold the Devil has on your family, marriage, money, or any other area drops off right now in Jesus' name. Amen.

AFTERWORD

This book is for people going through extremely challenging situations, situations for which there is no easy answer.

Here are six things you can keep in your spirit and use to walk through the darkest time of your life and come out on top:

Understand That God Is Good: God is not the author of the problem; He is your way out of the problem. While the Devil wants to defeat you and drive you away from God, you need to run toward God. God is good.

Don't Beat Yourself Up: You're not going through a difficult time because you're a bad person. You're experiencing difficulty because there's a Devil, and the Bible says the earth lieth in wickedness. Even if something is your fault, God can make up for your error if you allow Him.

Your Life Has Tremendous Value: You are the best idea God ever had. You're made in the image and likeness of God. You are here for a reason, and you are needed here.

Surround Yourself with The Word of God: Listening to anointed preaching brings strength to your body. Surround yourself with the Word of God and allow it to stir your spirit.

You Need to Be Around Conquerors: Don't seek the counsel of people going through the same problem. Find people who have conquered situations like your own and allow their testimony to inspire you to come out of your own situation.

All Things Will Work Together for Good: All things will work together for the good of those who love God and are called according to His purpose. This doesn't mean God causes the problems. It simply means He will use the problems for your good if you allow Him.

Maybe you are reading this, and you haven't received Jesus Christ as your Lord and Savior. It's the best decision you will ever make and a necessary step in overcoming your darkest time. It's a decision that will impact your marriage, your children, and the future generations to come.

Say this prayer out loud:

Heavenly Father, forgive me of my sins. I accept Jesus Christ as my Lord and Savior. I believe You sent Your son Jesus to die on the cross and that You raised Him from the dead on the third day so I can live free from sin, sickness, and poverty. Thank You God, for your forgiveness. Thank You for making me a part of Your family. I will never be the same again. I will honor You by committing my life to Your Word and to my family. I pray this in the name of Jesus, amen.

"MY GENERATION SHALL BE SAVED!"

— JONATHAN SHUTTLESWORTH

ABOUT THE AUTHOR

Evangelist and Pastor, Jonathan Shuttlesworth, is the founder of Revival Today and Pastor of Revival Today Church, ministries dedicated to reaching lost and hurting people with The Gospel of Jesus Christ.

In fulfilling his calling, Jonathan Shuttlesworth has conducted meetings and open-air crusades throughout North America, India, the Caribbean, and Central and South Africa.

Revival Today Church was launched in 2022 as a soul-winning, Holy Spirit-honoring church that is unapologetic about believing the Bible to bless families and nations.

Each day thousands of lives are impacted globally through Revival Today Broadcasting and Revival Today Church, located in Pittsburgh, Pennsylvania.

While methods may change, Revival Today's heartbeat remains for the lost, providing biblical teaching on faith, healing, prosperity, freedom from sin, and living a victorious life.

If you need help or would like to partner with Revival Today to see this generation and nation transformed through The Gospel, follow these links...

www.RevivalToday.com
www.RevivalTodayChurch.com

Get access to our 24/7 network Revival Today Global Broadcast. Download the Revival Today app in your Apple App Store or Google Play Store. Watch live on Apple TV, Roku, Amazon Fire TV, and Android TV.

Call: 412-787-2578

facebook.com/revivaltoday
x.com/jdshuttlesworth
instagram.com/jdshuttlesworth
youtube.com/@jonathanshuttlesworth

MY GENERATION SHALL BE SAVED

SANCTUS VITA

DO SOMETHING TODAY THAT WILL CHANGE YOUR LIFE FOREVER

THUS SAITH THE LORD, **MAKE THIS VALLEY FULL OF DITCHES**. FOR THUS SAITH THE LORD, YE SHALL NOT SEE WIND, NEITHER SHALL YE SEE RAIN; YET THAT VALLEY SHALL BE FILLED WITH WATER... **THIS IS BUT A LIGHT THING IN THE SIGHT OF THE LORD**... AND IT CAME TO PASS... **THE COUNTRY WAS FILLED WITH WATER.**

2 KINGS 3:16-18; 20

Revival is the only answer to the problems of this country - nothing more, nothing less, nothing else.

Thank you for standing with me as a partner with Revival Today. We must see this nation shaken by the power of God.

You cannot ask God to bless you first, prior to giving. God asks you to step out first in your giving - and then He makes it rain. We are believing God for 1,000 people to partner with us monthly at $84. Something everyone can do, but a significant seed that will connect you to the rainmaker.

IF YOU HAVE NOT YET PART-NERED WITH REVIVAL TODAY, JOIN US TODAY!

This year is not your year to dig small ditches. When I grew tired of small meetings and altar calls, I moved forward in faith and God responded. God is the rainmaker, but you must give Him something to fill. It's time for you to move forward! Will you stand with me today to see the nations of the world shaken by the power of God?

Revivaltoday.com/give

PayPal
revivaltoday.com/paypal

S Cash App $RTgive

venmo @RTgive

Text "RT" to 50155
Call at (412) 787-2578

Mail a check to:

Revival Today P.O. BOX 7
PROSPERITY PA 15329

REVIVAL TODAY   Email: info@revivaltoday.com